SCRUM
QUICKSTART GUIDE

A SIMPLIFIED BEGINNER'S GUIDE TO MASTERING SCRUM

ED STARK

Copyright © 2014 Ed Stark

ClydeBank Publishing

All rights reserved.

ISBN-13 : 978-1502771407

CONTENTS

7 - 9	Introduction
10 - 16	| 1 | Agile Project Management
17 - 22	| 2 | Agile Methodologies
23 - 27	| 3 | An Outline of Scrum
28 - 34	| 4 | A Discussion of Scrum Tactics
35 - 43	| 5 | Staff Implications of Scrum
44 - 48	| 6 | Operational Implications of Scrum
49 - 52	| 7 | Case Study #1 : Apple
53 - 58	| 8 | Case Study #2 : Google
59 - 62	| 9 | Case Study #3 : Santander
63 - 65	| 10 | Industry and Resources
66 - 68	Conclusion
69	About the Author
70 - 81	Preview of "Agile Project Management QuickStart Guide"
82	More Books by Ed Stark

INTRODUCTION

Project management is a part of the modern corporate environment. Those who are responsible fort the management of other staff or for the output of temporary or more ongoing project may be aware that there are different methods available to them, such as Scrum or DSDM. Others may have experience o the broader, more extensive business management strategies, such as Lean or Six Sigma. However, these terms may appear as obscure or barely familiar to some, merely catchwords that someone once used in a seminar or which they vaguely recollect from their university days.

The risk in discussing such terms, also, is that some people may not set much store by them, or may regard them with suspicion or hostility. Traditional management methods, especially where these are supposed to form part of "company culture". Are adhered to loyally, and defended vehemently. Such persons may also benefit from a deeper understanding of alternative strategies, though. The globalized international economy requires more immediate responses to shifting market circumstances. Technology which is marketed in staged introduction (something which is typical of the IT sector), or which needs to be introduced to the market in a very short space of time, may be more easily developed and perfected through the use of a more flexible, adaptable management system or project execution process.

In the contemporary commercial environment, where management has been extrapolated into an academic discipline and different paid consultants try to peddle their respective systems, managers should be as widely aware as possible of what is on offer and how it (or may not) be suitable to their specific purposes. Scrum represents one such alternative strategy, as a member of the Agile family of methodologies. In its approach the management of new product development, it operates in an inverse style to the more traditional structured, predetermined systems such as Waterfall.

Comparisons between such differing systems are important in assessing how a project should be approached. The success of Agile methodologies, and more importantly in this text, Scrum, indicates that management should take these approaches seriously, and attempt to at least understand them, so that if they still refuse to adopt them, even in isolated instances, they may yet be able to justify that rejection, instead of resorting tan unenlightened posture behind excuses of tradition or corporate culture, neither of which are marketable products.

On the contrary, the4 adoption of a more recent management style has been effected with enormous success by some of the largest enterprises in the IT industry. The presence per se of these management systems within the operations of these companies has turned out to be a talking point of its own, and a possible feature in the advertisement of their brands, or the recruitment of sought-after staff. In remaining relevant in today's market, it is, once again, imperative that management examines unfamiliar strategies.

This book does not attempt to make any sort of comparison between different management systems, besides very cursory comments to that effect. It merely explains Scrum, as a system, in its own right and also as a member of the Agile movement. Comparisons are common in industry literature and debates, and it remains the responsibility of the reader to determine which approach they prefer for operational reasons. It should be stated at the outset that there are now "correct" selections in this regard, but then the manager cannot institute a proper selection process if they are no equipped with adequate understanding of their several options.

CHAPTER ONE
Agile Project Management

People who have experience of Scrum or who make use of it sometimes may not always realize that it is, in fact, a subsidiary methodology of the Agile management philosophy. Although they may be aware of Agile, and may even have had some training in it, they may not understand the extent to which Scrum and Agile are related, or that Agile endows Scrum with some of its techniques. Understanding Agile is important in realizing the full potential of Scrum, since there is obviously a difference between merely doing what you are told to, or what everyone else has always done, and applying a more substantial insight in an attempt to modify or adapt (i.e. optimize) the existing management protocol.

Those who use Scrum should not have any difficulty in understanding how Agile operates, or what its priorities are. It is no less modern, having been established in the early 2000s, and it is also no less popular. It should be remembered at all times, though, that Agile is regarded as the overarching philosophy, of which Scrum is merely one methodology. Awareness of the other methodologies may also lead to the discovery that one or more of them may be better suited to certain projects, or that they contain tactics which are transferable to the reader's present management environment.

This chapter discusses Agile, starting with the history if its development, and then turning to its interior principles, and ending with a list of the subsidiary methodologies that it entails, such as Scrum.

History

Agile Project Management, as a management philosophy, originated in the IT sector. It is therefore most closely associated with that sector in the literature, and analysts also like to emphasize that point, sometimes critically so. However, it does have a broader application other industries and as such it s important fort managers or team leaders in any industry to understand how it operates and where it can potentially be of use to them.

In 2001, 17 of the most respected, prominent software developers conducted a meeting in the USA in order to determine an improved, more suitable management method for the development of new software. They launched this initiative in response to dissatisfaction with existing methods, and the perceived inability of the latter to accommodate the unstable, unpredictable environment in which software is developed.

Software development is seen as a precarious environment because it is always associated with what is known as " uncertainty". Uncertainty refers to the way that the final product cannot be described with certainty, because it can only be approved once the customer is using it and has expressed their satisfaction with it. Software needs to be tested before it can be accepted and used by its end-user. Also, some customers may experience difficulty in trying to describe what exactly they want the developer to give them, or what functionality the final product should have. Agile serves to limit or negate entirely the risks associated with this phenomenon.

Other management strategies, such as Waterfall, are not immune to uncertainty. In Waterfall, the entire development process is pre-planned, and implemented on a sequential, cumulative basis. Therefore, any trouble with a prior stage of the development scuppers the entire project, and leads to an potentially enormous waste of time and work. Also, Waterfall assumes that everything always happens according to plan, and this is obviously not sensitive in an environment which entails o much unpredictable feedback or such easily shifting expectations. (Waterfall is a rival management style, one which is often compared to Agile, and it has its own supporters, who in turn who their own reasons as to why it is superior to Agile, or anything else, for that matter). The participants at the meeting, some of whom are still publishing material management or have their own sites devoted to their specific refinements of Agile, styled themselves the Agile Alliance, and the conglomerate still exists at present.

Principles of Agile

Turning to the actual debate that arose during he meeting in 2001, the following problems with existing management processes were identified. They were termed "flawed assumption".

- The first flawed assumption is that it is possible to plan such a large project.

- The second flawed assumption is that it is possible to protect against late changes.

- The third flawed assumption is that it even makes sense to lock in big projects early.

Those at the meting then formulated 4 principles that they deemed to be more important than any other, principles on which to base their new management system these are:

- Individuals and interactions over processes and tools
- Working software over comprehensive documentation
- Customer collaboration over contract negotiation
- Responding to change over following a plan

As the reader may observe from examining these principles, the ere is an inherent and deliberate departure from the more process-driven, premeditated approach of Waterfall (or other systems). In expressing these 4 principles in practice, the developers composed 12 secondary principles which are supposed to be use to guide projects, in the sense of a guidebook or advisory framework. These are:

12 Principles of Agile Software:

- Our highest priority is to satisfy the customer through early and continuous delivery of valuable software.
- Welcome changing requirements, even late in development. Agile processes harness change for the customer's competitive advantage.
- Deliver working software frequently, from a couple of weeks to a couple of months, with a preference to the shorter timescale.
- Business people and developers must work together daily throughout

the project.

- Build projects around motivated individuals. Give them the environment and support they need, and trust them to get the job done.
- The most efficient and effective method of conveying information to and within a development team is face-to-face conversation.
- Working software is the primary measure of progress.
- Agile processes promote sustainable development. The sponsors, developers, and users should be able to maintain a constant pace indefinitely.
- Continuous attention to technical excellence and good design enhances agility.
- Simplicity – the art of maximizing the amount of work not done – is essential.
- The best architectures, requirements, and designs emerge from self-organizing teams.
- At regular intervals, the team reflects on how to become more effective, then tunes and adjusts its behavior accordingly.

(www.agilemanifesto.org)

Analysis of Methodology

Reading the raw principles quoted above may not provide the reader with any deeper insight into how Agile works. However, this section explains how Agile is applied in practice, and the reader should then be able to realize how it differs from other systems, and how it is potentially more advantageous.

To start with, Agile is what is known as iterative. Those familiar with Scrum may recognize this term. It simply means that the project progresses in stages, or iterations. However, at the end if each iteration in Agile the customer is presented with as usable output. They can therefore opt to terminate the project at that time. There is no obligation to continue with it, since the output or "vertical slice" is a workable product, and one that they may already be able to apply satisfactorily in their operations.

These vertical slices may be seen as layers on a cake. There is no rule according to which a cake should have more than one layer. So, a customer who has specified a 10-layer or 10-tier cake may eventually decide, after they have received 5 layers, that they are satisfied. The 5-layer cake is adequate for the wedding or party, and since their budget has suddenly been adjusted downwards, or the bride has changed her mind, they don't need the other 5 layers any more.

Agile allows this real-time, immediate adjustment of the project and its outcomes. This is the reason for its name, since it is able to adapt or respond immediately to changing circumstances or requirements. It is therefore flexible, and responsive. The fact that it happens in stages also means that it is incremental in nature, since the product is developed in increments.

The comparison of Agile to other, older management systems can be summarized in the following table. Note the different terminology. Agile does not try to be prescriptive or rigid Rather, it attempt to be as responsive as possible to the shifting expectations of the customer, which may in turn be based on market conditions or operational requirements.

Subsidiary Methodologies

These are the more refined, somewhat divergent subsystems that fall under the Agile umbrella. Some of them are suited to different environment or purposes, and some of them were not originally part of Agile, since they pre-date it. They may, in turn, have their own histories or specific tactics, but they are all similar in that they share the Agile philosophy, and they are therefore classed as components of its entire framework.

- Scrum
- Lean
- Crystal
- DSDM
- XP (or XProgramming – not the Microsoft operating system)

As the reader may be aware, Lean is actually a broader operational management philosophy, which has been adapted under the Agile heading, while DSDM is older than Agile and has an independent origin. Crystal and XProgramming are the systems of two of the contributors in the Agile Alliance, and pertain specifically to software development.

CHAPTER TWO
Agile Methodologies

It is necessary to discuss the other subsystems in detail, since the reader should be able to research them further from the list provided in Chapter 1. It is important that they do so, since these subsystems are not identical, and sometimes one or the other may be more suitable to the specific project that the reader is managing.

The 5 subsystems or methodologies described in this chapter do not represent an exhaustive list, nor are they necessarily always the most suitable for any particular project. But they are among the most prominent, and further research may lead the reader to encounter them anyway, especially where the reader is involved exclusively in the development of software.

Lean

Lean is a business management philosophy taken from the Japanese manufacturing sector. Initiated and perfected by the motor manufacturer Toyota, it is sometimes referred to as Toyotism. However, it is no less applicable top any organization anywhere else in the world, and is an example of how Japanese management practices have been assimilated into organizational strategy in other countries. Other examples of this phenomenon are Kaizen and JIT (Just-In-Time).

Lean operates on the premise that the waste in a process needs to be eliminated or reduced to its minimum possible extent. Waste I seen as anything that does not result in an addition of value to the output. For example, if someone is baking a cake, waste would be the power that is used by the oven if they leave it on for too long, since the cake can continue to bake using the residual heat of the appliance once it has been switched off. Or it may also be the use of excessive spice in the dough, since the customer won't be able to recognize the absence of the excess.

Lean entails a system of classification of the different types of waste that it seeks to eliminate. It uses Japanese terms to identify them, such as muda, mura and muri. In English, these refer to concepts such as time, input materials and, in Lean Six Sigma, the expertise of staff (such as where a highly qualified employee is performing more menial tasks). Lean has obvious practical implications for the organizations who use it. By reducing input costs, it serves to maximize the return on the process. It also causes an increase in processing speed, which is one of its objectives. The process should happen at maximum speed, or velocity. Time is seen as excessive processing time is seen as waste, so the Lean methodology accelerates the turnaround time on providing the customer what their desired output.

Insofar as Lean can be incorporated in Agile subsystems, it does not represent an independent methodology. Its primary philosophy is obviously of importance to anyone who manages a project or organization, and so managers are advised to study its precepts and try to apply them as and when they are able to.

DSDM

DSDM (Dynamic Systems Development Method) is an older methodology that was developed in the mid-1990s. It is used in the corporate sphere, and it is regarded by some, as being very "business-orientated", since it was, apparently, devised by people involved in commercial activity, and is therefore focused on their priorities and environment.

DSDM makes use of some management tools which may already be familiar to the reader. These are:

- Facilitated Workshops
- Modeling and Iterative Development
- MoSCoW Prioritization
- Timeboxing

(www.dsdm.org)

A possible criticism of DSDM is that a concept such as time-boxing is relatively more prescriptive that Agile is what Agile is usually associated with. Also DSDM is heavily administrative, in that it requires extensive pre-project studies and documentation. It also uses the concept of a consortium, who administer the documentation and provide it to the customer at a charge.

For those who desire to escape the more rigid, plan-orientated approach of Waterfall, but who are wary of the almost entirely flexible, seemingly improvisatory nature of Agile, DSDM may be a workable alternative, in that it provides a framework for the project, including formalized studies and paperwork.

Crystal

This is a programming methodology, i.e. it is used to develop software. Crystal is the brainchild of one of the original Agile Alliance members, and it is represented on the internet on his own website. Crystal places a substantial emphasis on quality. This involves the extensive testing of the new software, sometimes so much so that there is a team member dedicated to this function only. Its main proponent, Alistair Cockburn, lists the following principles as essential on his site:

- Human-powered: maximizing the potential of each person on the project team (people-centric as opposed to other-centric)

- Ultralight: the least possible administration and auxiliary activities, regardless of project size or scope

- Stretch-to-fit: always start out with a little less than you need and expand it to requirements (prevents wastage or "cutting away")

(www.alistair.cockburn.us)

A possible detraction of Crystal is that it involves so much testing, and to employ a team member solely on that basis is sometimes not feasible for some projects. However, thee elimination of errors in software is important, and the iterative approach of Agile allows them to be identified early and corrected, rather than to cause severe problems later, when the architecture of the software has been established and its more advanced functions are dependent on the sound operating of the the earlier stages.

XProgramming (Extreme Programming)

This is the project of another member of the Agile Alliance, Kent Beck. He, too, has a site dedicated to it. The reader should note that it has no relation whatsoever to the Microsoft XP operating system. XProgramming is the most commonly used methodology in software development in the USA at this time. It emphasizes two aspects of the process: quality, and constant interaction with the client. On the site, the following text appears: "Extreme Programming is a discipline of software development based on values of simplicity, communication, feedback, courage, & respect." The following "Core Practices" are outlined:

> *"Extreme Programming is a discipline of software development based on values of simplicity, communication, feedback, courage, & respect."*

Whole Team

- Planning Game, Small Releases, Customer Tests

- Simple Design, Pair Programming, Test-Driven Development, Design Improvement

- Continuous Integration, Collective Code Ownership, Coding Standard

- Metaphor, Sustainable Pace

(www.xprogramming.com)

Quality is administered and ensured through the use of system known as "peer programming", in which two programmer work in tandem and check each other's work. This practice is not universally popular, but it is very common, and is usually adopted by those who experiment with it.

Client interaction and feedback is also very important in XProgramming, sometimes to an extent that has been criticized. If the client is always on the premises, or is witness to the actual development process, this may have certain consequences, such as heightened or more immediate dissatisfaction, not necessarily with the product but with methods deployed in developing it, or simply as a result of the client's presence at the time of development and that they were able to influence the process. This intimate, ongoing presence and interaction needs to be managed with the prerequisite maturity and prudence, on the part of both parties in the interaction.

Those who manage software development projects may be particularly interested in this methodology, and should spend some time researching it.

CHAPTER THREE

An Outline of Scrum

The previous chapter (Chapter 2) described 4 of the most prominent Agile subsystems or methodologies. Scrum is another such methodology, and as the topic of this e-book it has been given its own chapter. It should also be noted that Scrum, in itself, represents a pristine example of the Agile approach generally, and as such it may be used to illustrate the principles and nature of any of the others. As an introduction to Agile, it is an extremely suitable alternative.

Scrum was developed by Ken Schwaber and Jeff Sutherland, two members of the Agile Alliance. Sutherland has stated that Scrum was originally initiated in 1993, but as one of the members of the Agile Alliance his management system has a natural affiliation with the Agile movement and is one of its primary methodologies. According to Sutherland, Scrum derives substantially from Japanese management systems, especially Lean.

The name "Scrum" derives from the sport of rugby, which is played in countries such as England, the antipodes and South Africa, as well as South America. It is very similar to American Football (NFL), and so the concept of a "scrum" should not be hard to understand for readers in the USA either.

A scrum occurs where the two teams are contesting possession of the ball. It is a set-piece movement, i.e. it is deliberately structured. The two teams use their eight players each, and arrange themselves in a traditional formation. They then apply pressure from opposite sides, in order to to overthrow the other team, or cause them to backpedal. The ball is tossed into the center of the scrum, at ground level, and the team whose "throw-in" it is usually secures possession by "hooking" the ball away from the other team (the number 2 player, or hooker, which is a specialist position in rugby and is not related to prostitution, hooks the ball under the feet of his team-mates by using one of his own).

The players who are involved in the scrum are the two props (jersey numbers 1 and 3; they are positioned on either side of the front, the hooker, the two locks (4 and 5; they form the second row, and the flanks (6 and 7), who form the third row of the formation. The eighth man (8, naturally) also forms part of the back row, but does not always remain there, and may break away once the scrum starts to fall apart, or for some other tactical reason. The player who throws the ball into the formation is the scrumhalf (9).

The name "Scrum" is therefore appropriate, in that it connotes intensive activity, the application of serious pressure or exertion to the tasks of the project, and, very importantly, a team effort. The collective nature of the scrum maneuver is so important that where a player who participates in the formation is sent off the field, he is immediately replaced by someone who plays in his position, at the expense of another player in the team who is not involved in the scrum. It is impossible for a team to scrum properly without using all eight players in the formation. The collective human weight of the entire formation (the pack weight) is important in rugby, and may exceed one metric ton. A team who fields an inferior pack weight can be seriously compromised in the match (it is not uncommon for a prop to weigh more than 225lb, or 100kg).

Basic Strategy

The basic premise of Scrum is that it involves a project team, who are coordinated by the project team manager, or Scrum Master. The word coordinated is not inappropriate here, since he Scrum Master is not a manager per se, but merely ensures that he team has the necessary resources at their disposal, and they are informed of progress on the project and the customer's feedback. Scrum does not, therefore, use the principle of a superior authority figure or management position. This is something which has attracted criticism and will be discussed in Chapter 5, since it relates to the staff implications of the Scrum system.

Scrum is iterative, like the other Agile methodologies, in that it involves the production of the project output in stages, or increments. Each iteration is known as a "sprint". A sprint may be very short, lasting only a matter of days, or it may occupy up to 4 weeks, but not more than 30 days. This is in contrast to other project management systems, such as Waterfall, where the entire time-frame is determined before the project starts, and may be estimated at 6 months, or 2 years. The impact of such long-term, vague estimations has been discussed more completely in Chapter 4.

The team in a Scrum project consists of only three roles. These are:

- The Product Owner
- The Scrum Master
- The Development Team members

The Product Owner is not the customer. They are the person in the organization who oversees the entire project at a macro or overarching level. The Scrum Master serves as the liaison between them and the Development Team. However, neither the Product Owner nor the Scrum Master has the authority to micromanage or supervise the Team. The Team does as they please, as long as they are working actively towards the accomplishment of the project objectives. They assume responsibility for the technical or concrete nature of the project work and its completion.

Tactics

These are the activities or output that are unique tot he Scrum methodology, and which are used or produced in support of its operation. Some of these terms may be familiar to people who manage projects, or they may make sense to them once they are explained, since they may have been encountered in different forms under different names.

The project is initiated with a "Kick-off meeting". A rugby match starts with the kick-off, and so this term is self-explanatory. The project backlog is then determined. The backlog is that which has to be produced by the project, and refers tot eh concrete outcomes that are expected by the customer, or anything else that the Team has to accomplish. The Sprints are then outlined.

A sprint is started with a Sprint Review meeting, during which the

Sprint Goal is determined. The Sprint Goal is the output that is envisaged for that particular sprint.

Every day, the Team conducts a Standup meeting. It should be apparent from this approach that immediacy and flexibility are the primary priorities in Agile. The Team is always aware of how much progress they have made in the project, what the customer's feedback has been, and whether they are potentially straying from the project focus or they have developed errors in the work. Meeting every 24 hours on this basis, in an intensive, employee-driven environment of only 15 minutes, prevents the possibility of protracted, tedious meetings during which senior executives obfuscate unsatisfactory figures or try to assign blame for detected errors.

The output of Scrum, such as the Release, the backlog list and the burndown chart, are known as its artifacts. The Release is the eventual, final product offerings, as delivered tot he customer, as opposed to the iterative output of each Sprint which is known as the Increment. The backlog list is, obviously the list of project objectives, and th or things which the Team has to accomplish, and the burndown chart is a descending graph with time on its X-axis, which illustrates the progress of the project generally.

CHAPTER FOUR

A Discussion of Scrum Tactics

In order to apply Scrum, people need to understand how its different tactics or methods operate, and how they should be structured. This requires that they understand the purposes served by each tactic, so that they are able to implement it within the broader framework of the project, as managed by the Scrum overarching methodology. Ostensibly frivolous or trivial terms and activities, such as standing during the daily meeting or limiting the Sprints to a relatively short time period, start to make sense once they are viewed in the context of the entire methodology.

Generally speaking, the main priorities in the physical application of Scrum are described by the 3 "pillars" or precepts of its operation. These are"

- Transparency
- Inspection
- Adaptation

Transparency refers tot he way that everyone involved in the project is required have a proper understanding of its objectives and progress. This extends to the customer, and other less implicated observers, such as industry watchdogs or government authorities. Transparency relies on the other two precepts for its maintenance.

Inspection entails the monitoring of the project work in order to ensue that it remains material to the objectives, or backlog. This is an obvious part of project management, and won't be surprising or even unfamiliar to those who have experience of project management. Adaptation is based on Inspection, and is occasioned as a result of negative assessment, such as when the Team is deviating from the Sprint Goal or the customer determines that the product is not going to meet their specified requirements. The main tactics all serve these 3 precepts, and they are discussed below, each under its own heading. They have been mentioned in Chapter 3, and they are now elaborated on to enhance the reader's insight into them and ability to deploy them as required. Sometimes, these tactics are referred to as Scrum Events, and this is also the term used in the official Scrum documentation.

Sprint Planning

This Event takes place at the outset of a Sprint. It is not supposed to last longer than 8 hours, and that maximum duration applies to a relatively longer Sprint, such as one of a month. During this meeting, the Scrum Team (which consists of the Product Owner, the Scrum Master and the Development Team) determine what the Product Backlog list entails . These are the items of output that need to be delivered in order to complete the project. They then formulate the Sprint Goal around this list.

Sprint Planning therefore aims at answering two questions, or resolving two issues. Firstly, what is needed? What material outcomes is the Sprint supposed to achieve. Secondly, how are these outcomes going to be realized?

Note that a Sprint Planning Event can pertain to either an entire project, where the project consists of only one Sprint, or merely to a Sprint within the entirety of the broader project. The Scrum Team therefore decides on the Increment that is to be delivered at the end of the Sprint, but this may not always be so, since the Increment may be the sole project outcome and as such the project consists of only one Sprint.

Daily Scrum

As mentioned in Chapter 3, this is the daily meeting that the Development Team undertakes to assess their progress. During this meeting, which is known as the Daily Scrum, the team is not allowed to sit down,ad n the meeting does not last longer than a quarter of an hour. The following questions are addressed:

- What did I achieve yesterday that relates to the Sprint Goal?
- What do I intend to do today that relates to the Sprint Goal?
- Are there any obstructions to the Team achieving the Sprint Goal?

This meeting is also known as a Standup Meeting, because participants are not allowed to be seated during its course. It is also not allowed to last more than 15 minutes.

Sprint Review

The Sprint Review is a meeting that takes place at the end of a Sprint. This meeting is extremely important in that it allows for the presence of other role-players, such as the customer. These are invited by the Product Owner. This meeting is not allowed to last more than 4 hours, and Sprints shorter than 1 month it may even be shorter.

During this meeting, the Scrum Team and the other role-players thrash out the details of what was achieved during the Sprint, how it affects the Product Backlog (i.e. the required project outcomes) and whether any adaptation of the latter is necessary. This approach emphasizes the priority of Agile that flexibility and immediate responses are necessary in ensuring satisfactory product output and customer satisfaction. By delivering the final product in Increments, or iteratively, the customer has more control over the development process and is better able to influence it. Also, preliminary errors are easier to eliminate and the quality or functionality of the finished item is generally more likely.

Sprint Retrospective

The purpose of the Sprint Retrospective is to:

- Inspect how the last Sprint went with regards to people, relationships, process, and tools;
- Identify and order the major items that went well and potential improvements; and,
- Create a plan for implementing improvements to the way the Scrum Team does its work.

This is a broader assessment which is conducted by the Scrum Team only. During this meeting, they assess their performance during the Sprint and try to determine whether they are able to improve somehow, or whether the Team itself needs to be adapted. This is therefore an introspective Event which focuses on the actual Team and project management process, and may result in more general conclusions that those related to the specific concrete project of which the Sprint was a part.

Meetings such as these are not always easy to conduct, since they may include criticism of certain members' work or the exposure of negative relations and tension within the team. That is why, by having them on such a regular basis, the Scrum system does not allow for these issues to accumulate or feaster, and therefore enables them to be resolved or removed in a much shorter space of time than other, more traditional management systems. It also demonstrates how the Agile approach prioritizes human interaction and the promotion of constant communication. This makes it much harder for secondary issues to impact negatively on the project work, or delay the delivery of the final outcome.

Scrum Artifacts

These are the concrete output of the project and its management process. They need to be mentioned because they are related to the Events described above and because they are used in the operation of the latter. The reader should take note that the Artifacts are of two types:

- Those which are used in the management of the project
- Those which are delivered tot he customer, i.e. the product itself

They are both termed as Artifacts so the distinction is important to remember.

Product Backlog

This is a list of the customer's requirements or expectations, of or for the finished item. The Backlog list contains all the specifications or features that need to be achieved. Using the example of the cake again, the customer may specify that the cake is:

- 3 tiers high
- Made with chocolate dough
- Iced in white
- Inclusive of a national flag design on its upper surface

Sprint Backlog

These are the items of output that need to be achieved during the present Sprint. They therefore for part of the entire project's output, but they also lead to a usable increment in their own right.

In baking the cake, the Development Team might identify the mixing of the dough as their Sprint Backlog item. They can then break that priority down further into its constituent activities, such as purchasing the ingredients for the dough, measuring them, sifting the flour, and generally mixing the dough until it is usable in making the cake.

Note that the outcome of the Sprint provides a usable Increment, i.e. the dough. If the customer runs out of funds, or they no longer require the cake, the dough is not wasted. They can pay the Developers for the dough and then store it or apply it to some other purpose in future. This is a central principle in Agile management, as opposed to a system such as Waterfall which would entail the baking of the entire cake before anything was presented to the customer, and sometimes in the entire absence of customer monitoring or feedback, so that a customer who exhausted their funds prior to that would be left with, to use standard cliché, a half-baked project outcome.

Increment

The Increment is the physical product output of the Sprint, such as the dough mentioned the previous section.

Monitoring Aids

These are the administrative items that the Team uses to monitor and analyze their progress. Some of them may be fairly standard in project management, such as burndown or flow charts, and there is potentially no limit on what the Scrum Master or Product Owner can use in this regard. However, the important point to remember here is that the administration of the project should not have a negative effect on its progress, in keeping with the principles of Agile, and Scrum as well. Such measures should be kept to a minimum, and should be understood by everyone involved. They should also be made easily available to anyone who requires them.

Done

This is an extremely important term in Scrum. It may seem self-explanatory or to plain to be so significant, but it is, because the methodology requires that all role-players understand what it entails. In other words, there needs to be absolute and universal consensus as to the specifications of the finished product, or what the precise expectations of the customer are, so that the project output can be properly assessed. The Scrum Team needs to agree on what Done refers to, so that they can structure their work and monitor their progress accordingly.

CHAPTER FIVE

Staff Implications of Scrum

As a system of project management, Scrum affects how staff are supervised and managed. This, in turn, relates to how they experience the system, the project generally, and also the relationships between individual members of staff and the issues that pertain that environment. Authority, cooperation and sound interaction are all items of discussion that are important in understanding how to implement Scrum, and what may possibly arise as an obstacle or point of dispute.

Hierarchy

This is sometimes a source of serious contention in any organization, regardless of what management system is in use. Some staff are naturally resistant to authority, or what they perceive as unnecessary supervision or (supposedly) unjustified superiority in status, while others are far more sensitive to authority and seek instruction in practically everything that they do, and are hesitant to operate without such input. Scrum has its own philosophy on team hierarchy and the assignment of responsibility, and this should be examined more closely by anyone who wishes to make use if it.

The acceptance and application of vertical authority is sometimes easier in more elaborately structured, inflexible organizational hierarchies, where the ability of individual staff to dissociate themselves from the tasks of others is far more substantial. In such management systems, staff usually have very specific, rigidly defined designations, or "job titles", and they may sometimes resort tot he assertion that a task "isn't part of their job description". Although this attitude is regarded as reprehensible, and the symptom of a lazy or under-performing employee, it is less possible in Scrum, for two main reasons.

The first is that the Scrum team is simply too small to allow for that type of irresponsibility or laissez-fair inclination to pass unnoticed or un-arrested. Where a small group of people collaborate on the same common purpose, it is very difficult for individual members to disengage even partially from their allotted portion of the team's work. It is not in human nature to permit such lack of enthusiasm, or shirking, yet this phenomenon is easier to hide ion larger organizations, where standard protocol or copious documentation may be deployed in an attempt to achieve that aim. As an example, an employee in a company that has advertised a stated turnaround time of 48 hours may insist on utilizing that time period, even though they are able to assist the customer the same day. Or they may deliver a progress report that is so lengthy or tech9inicaslly involved as to require several hours or presentation, and which contains highly massaged or excessively interpreted data that cast the employee's or entire team's performance in a more impressive light than it merits in reality.

The second reason is that the Development Team is cross-functional.

It therefore entails multiple skills, as required by the project brief, or Product Backlog. Cross-functionality implies that the members of the Team are interdependent on one another, i.e. they cannot perform their own tasks without the input of the other members. This in turn translates into a situation in which the failure of one or more members to meet the required performance standard impedes the entire project and is going to be detected immediately. The three questions that are asked during the Daily Scrum, such as what was achieved yesterday that assisted the accomplishment of the Sprint Goal, or what exists at present that may potentially obstruct that outcome, encompass this consideration.

Secondary reasons to the above two are that Scrum, as a member of the Agile family of methodologies, does not place its primary emphasis on paperwork, or administrative issues. As such, Team members cannot use documentation or procedure to isolate themselves from added responsibility, or to create the impression that they have achieved more than they have in reality. At the same time, the Scrum philosophy includes the concept of a Daily Scrum, where team members may raise and debate such observations, so they are potentially resolvable within 24 hours, unlike in massive institutions where employees may develop a professional strategy over their careers of accomplishing only the absolutely essential workload and providing only the bare minimum availability of their time to colleagues or customers. As an exercise in staff motivation, Scrum should therefore be considered as an alternative paradigm to the other motivational methods.

The positions in the Scrum system are:

Product Owner

This is the overarching project manager, or leader. The Product Owner manages the Product Backlog. They are responsible for it. They are only allowed to one person. They operate at a higher level in the organization than any one else involved in the project. They may be the only person who liaises with the client. They assign organizational resources to the project, and approve its initiation. The Scrum Master reports tot hem, but they also have contact with the Development Team during the Sprint Retrospective, i.e. The project meeting which is organized at th end of each Sprint. Their direct communication with the Team shows how Scrum encourages close cooperation between all role-players, regardless of their title or position in the organization. The Product Owner is also unable to dictate tot he Team how they perform the project work – it remains their sole responsibility.

Scrum Master

This role is sometimes misunderstood. The Scrum Master manages the performance of the Development Team, and facilitates their ease of progress, it is true, but on a broader, organizational level they are also responsible for the implementation of Scrum, and training or up-skilling other staff in its principles. They therefore have a more general role than mere team coordination or feedback distribution. The Scrum Master participates in abroad and extensive network of communication activities. They provide feedback tot he Product Owner, and they also train the Development Team (and anyone else, for that matter) in how Scrum operates and how to apply its principles. Note, tough, that they do not provide management or instructions on how to perform the physical project work. They merely ascertain that the progress of the work is appropriate to the Product Backlog or the Sprint Goal.

Development Team

These are the employees who perform the physical project work, in pursuit of the Product Backlog items, or, more specifically, that particular Sprint Goals. The team may vary in its composition from Sprint to Sprint, and may exist only for the sake a specific project. The Team is cross-functional, i.e. it is designed to incorporate all the skills that he project requires, and it is supposed to be relatively smaller (although this latter imperative is not observed by some very prominent adherents of Agile, such as Google. The Team has no internal hierarchy, and the only title is that of "Developer". The separate responsibilities of each Team member do not result in individual liability for non-performance. The latter is something that the entire Team assumes, should it arise.

Operational Attitudes

Employees sometimes express resistance to authority generally. They do not respect the authority of a superior employee, or they become demoralized by its application. This may be due to several reasons, such as the personal profile of each employee, in term so age, gender or social reputation, or due to more professional, technical circumstances, such as level of qualification, perceived degree of expertise, or length of service in the industry. All of these factors may cause subordinate staff to question or obstruct the ordinary course of institutional command and regulation.

An example here is the position of the Scrum Master. A point of criticism that has been raised about this position, is that it is too poorly defined, or vague. The Scrum Master does not participate in the project work, yet they have no authority to determine its progress or to give instructions to the Development Team. They act merely as a facilitator in the project process. Some staff may raise the question as to why the Scrum Master is necessary, or how their duties are so important as to require the establishment of a separate position in the management system. Another potential query relates to the fact that he Scrum Master does not perform the actual project work. This may result in Team members raising the age-old issue: "What does so-and-so actually do the whole day?"

Such issues are easily addressed by adherence to a policy of proper education. Before Scrum is implemented, all affected employees should understand how it operates and why it is suited to the project at hand, or how it it offers superior outcomes to their management systems. Each participant should have an adequate awareness of how they reside in the Scrum system and what is expected of them. In this way, the importance of each position will become apparent,l and the entire Scrum Team will be more amenable to titles such as Scrum Master or Product Owner, with which they may not be familiar or which they may not understand the full significance of.

The use of such terms, and the inclusion of tactics such as Standup Meetings, may seem strange to some employees per se. Incorporating the terminology of a foreign sport into project management, or conducting meetings without chairs in a quarter of an hour, may be easy for some staff to tolerate, especially those who have been employed in the organization for a long time and who set store by the more trusted, more traditional methods. They may express the opinion that Scrum is somehow "childish", "unprofessional" or "gimmicky", or not entirely orientated on the technical project tasks. Other employees may merely be disinterested due to the more usual de-motivation or inherent disloyalty that some staff experience in the course of their work.

Once again, these issues are best addressed through adequate education and training. All Team members should be aware of how Scrum is implemented, and how they are required to contribute to its success. They should also be informed that performance appraisal and remuneration system apply equally to the Scrum project as they would to ordinary duties.

Scrum is not a holiday philosophy, or an alternative, esoteric approach to projects. It is a de facto, legitimate management system and it is used by many enterprises. The provision of data on the history and prevalence of Scrum should assist in ensuring that staff understand that Scrum is no less serious than their more usual responsibilities and that it may even be of significant benefit tot eh company if they are prepared to assist in its implementation and success.

More traditional project management systems, such as Waterfall, or those used in large institutions employing hundreds of staff on one project, may suffer from issues of staff motivation or sustained commitment to the project. The attitude that there is always more time or that the deadline is inexorably distant may lead to some staff postponing obvious project activities or generally relinquishing their sense of dedication to the tasks that they are responsible for.

They may also not have a comprehensive understanding of what the entire project entails, or how its different elements interact in the delivery of the finished product to the customer. Being a member of such a massive or long-term project team may obscure such insights from ordinary employees, so that they are unable to maintain a holistic focus and they then start to apply minimal exertion to the isolated, disjointed tasks that they are indeed given to complete.

Scrum addresses both of these possible issues through its philosophy. The most obvious aspect of Scrum that is material to the first one is the maximum duration of an iteration, or Sprint. At 30 days, it does not allow employees to procrastinate endlessly or to lose the emphasis on consistent, project-orientated progress. Procrastination is a pet hate of motivational speakers, and the graph below portrays the relationship between the proximity of the deadline and the tendency of staff to engage in this practice.

In terms of the broader understanding of the project and its interior elements, Scrum prescribes the use and universal distribution of exact and collectively compiled documentation. A list such as the Product Backlog is composed by the entire team during the Kickoff Meeting, and so everyone in the Development Team nows what it entails and how its component items are supposed to be achieved. This availability and awareness of relevant information reflects the people-orientated nature of Scrum (and Agile generally), in that staff are accommodated through the provision and application of such information. Their need to possess a summary knowledge of the project, and more specifically how their own tasks, no matter how seemingly menial or temporary, fit into the entire process, should never be underestimated. Employees on the very lowest level of the organization may regard the successful completion of their duties as a matter of personal accomplishment, and so they should be made to feel included in the management of the project, since their input may not only be necessary, but innovative.

Generally speaking, this latter consequence is to be supported, since it is important in commerce and maintaining a competitive position in the market. By using smaller teams, and by giving team members such as ordinary employees such extensive responsibility over their tasks and technical strategies, Scrum serves to empower them, so that they are more able (as well as being openly encouraged) to take ownership of their output, in the context of a team environment where they are supported and assisted by those aiming at the same project objectives or Product or Sprint Backlog items.

This sense of ownership is essential in the motivation of staff and the improvement of their work. It is something that management may insist on sometimes, sometimes as a repetitive exhortation that eventually turns into a tedious refrain tot eh staff. However, by adjusting the entire management system to encourage this attitude among the ordinary workers, Scrum establishes an operational environment in which it is more likely to be assumed and applied, not through individual choice but operational necessity.

CHAPTER SIX

Operational Implications of Scrum

Expense and Time

Scrum has already been described as a system that is opposite in nature to the more traditional management systems, such as Waterfall. The primary divergence is that Scrum is iterative, and adjust as it progresses, whereas Waterfall is more inflexible, and once the preliminary planning has been done, it is much harder to deviate from the stated forecasting or published plan of work and progress. These two approaches entail certain implications for matters such as budget, time-frame and staff participation.

To start with, expense and turnaround time are usually calculated before the project is commenced. This process of prediction can be subject to vast estimation, and sometimes produces very vague, or even optimistic, results. An estimated time-frame may be as broad as "18 to 24 months", giving the impression that no-one involved in it is reliably sure as to how much time the project is eventually going to require. The project budget, too, may be so poorly defined as to be largely irrelevant in the final analysis.

This is obviously hazardous to the success of the project, because it may potentially destroy the enthusiasm of the customer, or render the project unfeasible as it progresses. It is also unsuitable to an environment in which new products need to be introduced to the market at very short (perhaps in response to a competitor's offering, or an identified error in an existing item), or where the market request something that has not yet been made available.

Exceeding budgetary and time constraints is always a risk in projects which focus exclusively on the desired final specifications of the output. Some enterprises are prepared to sustain such departures from forecasting, as long as they are able to attain the ultimate design. However, if that design fails commercially, their exorbitant expense and consumption of time cannot be justified on any grounds.

Scrum does not allow this to happen. Like the other Agile approaches, it is iterative, in that the project can be stalled or terminated after any Sprint (or iteration). The customer then receives a usable product, no matter how primordial it may be in relation to the final one. Therefore, if the customer's budget is exhausted, or the deadline shifts, or any other factor arises that causes a deviation from what has been planned for either of those two aspects of the project, the entire exercise is not a dead loss and the customer may yet be satisfied, even if only partially.

The summary point here is that it is far more difficult for Agile systems of management to exceed their budgets or time-frames. The inability to guarantee stricter adherence to estimated figures is a deterrent to new investment and is a traditionally notorious characteristic of structured, premeditated management systems such as Waterfall. The phenomenon of going over budget, or taking more time than was anticipated, while sometimes attracting a somewhat wry response, does not impress anyone, either in the industry or the market, and may even damage the service provider's reputation or cause the entire project to become financially unsound.

Quality

As stated throughout this text, Scrum is iterative, so the quality of the finished product, or any of its stages of development, is easier to assess and regulate. This may sound contrived, since the quality of work in progress can be checked in any project management system, but then it is not as empty an assertion as one may suspect. Long-term projects, especially those which consist of the development of complementary segments of the final item, sometimes allow errors or defects to slip in, since the latter cannot be detected until the final product is in use, or until a more advanced stage of development exposes them. However, by that time, it is too late to rectify them, and sometimes the entire architecture of the item has to be adjusted or, in extreme cases, constructed from scratch.

Scrum pre-empts this possibility, largely, through its principle of incremental development. Each "|slice" or stage of the final product is developed independently, and should be able to function on its own, or in conjunction with those already developed. It is therefore far less likely that an error of a systemic and /or relayed nature will be incorporated into the final output, since it will be detected much earlier and eliminated.

To sue the example of the cake, a system like Waterfall would require that the entire cake is baked and then presented to the customer. The latter then scrapes away some of the icing and discovers that there is no chocolate in the dough. It is pale vanilla dough. The entire cake is a disaster and the bakery cannot charge the customer for it. Their only option is to transport it back to their premises, at their expense, and hope that at some time in the next 72 hours someone else purchases it. This would not happen in Scrum, because the dough itself represents a Sprint. At the end of that Sprint, the dough would be checked for quality. The omission of the cocoa powder would be noticed immediately, and only the vanilla dough would be lost (or frozen in storage), or it could be re-mixed to suit the customer's specifications.

Customer Experience

Quality is immensely important in the development of new products. In the IT sector, Microsoft's Windows operating system once crashed, famously, during its public launch. Some customer may be prepared to accept budget overruns, longer time-frames or even additional specifications if the product performs to their requirements and, more importantly, does not present errors or malfunctions.

The use of an iterative approach ensures that the customer is always informed of the progress of the project. XProgramming takes this a step further, by prescribing the presence of the client representative at the development venue, to take a more interactive, involved role in assessment and commentary. Scrum, for its part, conducts the Sprint Review, where the customer is present and provides input on such matters.

Adhering to budget is also extremely important, as is meeting deadlines. This point does not need to be emphasized. Few, if any, companies command such significant market influence that they can afford to keep their customers waiting, either for a new product or for added features. The reliability generally of a service provider or product developer is an integral operational imperative, since quality is not able to compensate for a late market entry or unsustainable input costs.

CHAPTER SEVEN

Case Study #1 : Apple

Apple is an internationally known and reputable manufacturer of IT appliances, such as laptops and smartphones. The prime examples are the Mac (laptop or notebook) and the iPhone (a massively popular smartphone, which has been released in several successive versions). Apple also produces operating system software, including an office suite and a web browser. The company is one of the three main operating system development sources, together with Microsoft, which is also proprietary (Windows) and then the open source Linux family of systems. Apple is publicly listed and trades at about $350 per share. Former CEO, the late Steve Jobs, was regarded as a captain of industry and an inspirational figure, both in and outside of the IT sector.

Environment

Apple operates in an environment in which there is constant innovation and competition. The market for appliances or devices such as laptops and phones is gigantic, and is characterized by a prominent demand in the market for new technology or the latest features. Competition revolves around the introduction of new items or the refinement of existing specifications to make the product more attractive.

This technological elaboration and modification is accompanied by the need for improved or entirely new software, such as the next version of an operating system or the introduction of mobile phone apps. The development of new software is therefore of extreme importance to industry operators such as Apple, and the utilization of Scrum in the operations of the enterprise is hardly surprising.

Implementation

The implementation of Scrum by Apple, or Agile generally, illustrates the principles of the system,. These principles have been outlined by the description of how the company uses Agile to manage its development of new products. The terms and concepts should already be familiar to the reader.

Firstly, Apple streamlined their workforce considerably. 4000 staff at middle management level were eliminated, and lower-ranking staff were promoted to manageme4nt positions. This is in keeping with the notion of staff taking ownership of the development and production process themselves. In Scrum, they do not always need a supervisor, since such an position would either be extraneous or would impede the progress of the project work. This is one reason why the Scrum Master has such a periphery, unengaged role in the system. Secondly, Apple pre-empted the possibility of "shirking" or the evasion of responsibility, deliberate or otherwise, by implementing their own concept – that of the DRI (directly responsible individual). This concept, which may some very attractive to some frustrated managers, does not allow for employees to hide behind documentation or protocol. Once someone has been explicitly identified as responsible for a Backlog item, they cannot transfer that onus onto someone else, or use the project administration to obscure its outcome or absence.

Outcome

As stated in the chapter on operational implications of Scrum (Chapter 6), the fact that new products can be developed in slices or iterations allows for them to be introduced on a staggered basis. This, in turn, pre-empts the development and marketing of potentially unsuccessful offerings, since a new product can be modified or even canceled in its preliminary stages. By making only the most basic (in effect, prototype) model available to the public, the developer can assess the response of the latter and decide as to whether it is worth pursuing further development or promotion.

Contrary to what some people may believe, the IT industry is not immune to failed products. Specific niche uses do not always translate into mass marketability, while some technology is refined to an advanced extent too late to be of use, since ti is entirely replaced by a newer, more attractive option. An example would be the "floppy" disks that people used in the 1990s. The earliest floppy disk had a capacity of between 360KB and 1.44MB. Such disk were eventually developed to the point where they could hold 120MB. However, the use of the last option was limited, since the medium is not structurally reliable (it loses data or becomes defective on its own, in the absence of obvious outside interference), and it was replaced by compact disk technology (CDs), and, later, DVDs), which are far more reliable and which hold a minimum of 700MB at the same price, not to mention vastly superior processing speed.

In an environment in which constant innovation is required, not merely to maintain market share but to remain relevant in the sector, Scrum offers companies like Apple the opportunity to fragment or dilute the expense of new development. R&D (research and development) is sometimes seen as a sunk cost in the establishment of new products, in any industry, so Scrum enables cheaper solutions in that respect, and also the earlier abandonment of suspected unfeasible products or activities.

This demonstrates how the Agile philosophy allows much faster response to the market's opinion or the difficulties that a product may encounter during its development and introduction. Such development then becomes less of a gamble, and is not a "shot in the dark" or a bold statement of confidence" any more, since it is more reliant on practical experience and concrete feedback than hypothetical forecasts, no matter how carefully considered or expert, and the possibly hubris (or desperate) ambitions of embattled management executives or intransigent operatives who are excessively loyal to a product or market strategy.

CHAPTER EIGHT

Case Studey #2 : Google

Google is the most prominent search engine in most countries that use the internet. With the exception of China, where it is in competition with domestic operators who are protected by the local government and censorships policies, Google is the traditionally used engine by all internet users, to the extent that its name has become an ordinary word in everyday English. To Google something means to search for it online.

Besides its search engine business, which was its initial market offering, Google has also expanded its operations to include a web browser (Chrome) and a mobile phone operating system (Android). The free e-mail service Gmail remains one of the most popular such services on the internet. Various periphery services such as translation, document editing and file storage are also provided.Subsidiary operations entail YouTube, the largest online video sharing site, and GooglePlus, or Google+, a social networking and media site, similar to Facebook or MySpace, but using different concepts and terminology.

Environment

Google therefore requires that its software remains absolutely reliable and contemporary. Its user base and traffic frequency are so high that these requirement are not negotiable. The site is used to perform in excess of 1 trillion searches annually. That equates to approximately 3 billion per day. It is obvious from these figures that it is not merely being used for entertainment or leisure. Commercial enterprises rely on Google to support or maintain their ordinary operations, and the search engine also enables the easy access and retrieval of information that is not available to people locally in some other form. The other services, particularly Gmail, provide communication solutions to those whoa re unable to afford their own online server or who cannot rely on an their own infrastructure because they are too mobile or remotely based.

It is customary for search engines to use advertising to generate revenue. This advertising, which is sometimes referred to as targeted advertising, is typically located on the margins of the page that the user is viewing. It may be related to the search topic, or the subject matter in the user's e-mails, as examples. Targeted advertising has been criticized in the past, because its formulation involves the analysis of the user's data, but it is nevertheless an entrenched feature of the niche in which Google operates.

Google's twin requirements of absolute reliability and undeviating immediacy of information require that the software it uses are always pristine and material to the environment in which its users operate. Because it is so internationally utilized, that market is rather large and amorphous, so the software should be universally usable and effective, at all times.,

One of the most important elements of that software is the search algorithm, or the technical paradigm that the engine uses to assess search terms and assign importance to websites. This algorithm is the source of much speculation and debate in related market sectors, and is updated on a constant basis. It is proprietary and is never released publicly, even though it remains the subject of acute speculation and discussion.

Implementation

One of the most noted feature s of Google's management system, is that it is relatively more informal than that observed in other organizations. Developers are permitted to dedicate a fifth of their time to personal projects or those which are not related to any operational issue. Google is, in fact, notorious for its more relaxed,   less institutional corporate culture and environment. Employees receive extensive perks, such as catering and gym facilities. Also, organizational hierarchy is not as much of a priority as it is in other enterprises. Authority is not defined and delegated in a strict, legislated architecture of power.

However, for the purposes of this case study, the most interesting aspect of this culture is the way that it mirrors Agile philosophy, particularly in its management of the development teams. In giving its managers imperatives to pursue in their positions, Google has identified certain key principles, as well as some important potential negative issues. These are summarized in a numbered list which the company has published publicly. Some of the items deserve more detailed discussion here, since they are either reconcilable with Agile (Scrum) doctrine or they mirror it to the extent that they may possibly have been inspired by or derived form it.

To start with, there is the instruction to "be a good coach". This is similar to the Scrum Master's priority of coordinating and motivating the Development Team in Scrum. Related to this item is the instruction not to micro-manage, something which Scrum prescribes, and which was mentioned in Chapter 3. Having a clear vision and strategy for the team, too, is linked to the concept of an established and universally understood Product Backlog list or Sprint Goal. All of these priorities are similar to or the same as those apparent in Scrum. It has been published that Google uses the Agile philosophy in its development processes, although not necessarily in the traditional, textbook fashion that some other companies may do (as an example, a Google development team may consist of thousands of programmers).

Outcome

The use of agile philosophy in the development of search engine software is significant in that the environment is amenable to this application of the former. The ability of Scrum to provide iterative or segmented improvements or refinements of the existing software infrastructure is important, because it enables the search engine operator to adapt immediately to shifts in market behavior or the introduction of new products or services by other service providers.

The internet is an incessantly changing, shifting commercial, social and operational environment in which new techniques, trends and material are the order of the day. As soon as a new tactic or phenomenon arises, Google needs to be able to accommodate it within its own operations, so as to minimize negative consequences and ensure that its own target market is satisfied with its service. Subsidiary sites such as YouTube or GooglePlus indicate a desire to respond to the initiatives of competitors, but the more inherent, sometimes insipid, tactics of various role-players online require that Google is able to meet the needs of its users as they arise.

An example would be the way that some sites, in earlier times, deployed a tactic known as "keyword stuffing" to elevate their status in search engine rankings. The basic principle behind this tactic is that search engines focus on the use of keywords on a site. For example, if a site is about apples, it should then contain that word as many times as possible in order to attract the attention of the search engines and rank higher in their results pages. Keyword stuffing then entails the deliberate and excessive presence of the keyword or phrase on the site, such as by including it thousands of times in the same color as the page background, rendering its otherwise pointless repetition invisible, or populating the site with unnatural, useless, obsessively repetitive text structured around that word. Search engines need to be savvy tot his type of attitude (which is known technically as "black hat SEO" or search engine optimization", as opposed to "white hat" tactics, which are approved of; hat colors are used to indicate the desirability or nature of software generally in the IT industry), and these days keyword stuffing is regarded by nefarious as Google and actually serves to reduce or eliminate the site's presence in the engine's results.

This shows that Scrum is a viable project management alternative in companies who employ thousands of staff and who operate in the most immediate, large-scale and unstable markets. It is even possible to assert that no other management system, besides those in the Agile family, would enjoy such success in that type of environment.

CHAPTER NINE

Case Study #3 : Santander

In order to demonstrate the more universal applicability of Scrum, and its successful deployment in an environment that is not necessarily IT related, this chapter discusses an example where the system is used in the management of non-IT projects. This is the stated approach of banking group Santander, who have operations in the USA and the UK. The financial services sector is heavily based on It, yet it also involves other operational environments, and as such its extreme emphasis on customer service, immaculate integrity of data and stringent institutional security present any management system with one its most severe tests in implementation. In addition those considerations, Santander is an international operator with a net income of approximately $1bn in 2013 and nearly 10 000 staff.

Environment

the financial services environment is extremely competitive, and also subject to intensive legislative regulation and potential sanction. Circumstances can change very suddenly in finance, such as when the IT network of an institution is compromised, or the governmental authorities in a country try to intervene in an impending financial disaster. Mass market shifts are not unheard of, and competition is ever present. The fact that several operators offer exactly the same products and services require them to be able to match rival offerings in the shortest possible space of time. The differentiation in brands encouraged by advertising cannot mitigate the need for urgent and effective introduction to the market where one player has devised a new offering, or improved an existing one.

The priority of data integrity should not be underestimated in this sector of the economy, either. The administration of personal and corporate finances is an immense responsibility and one which can only be satisfactorily discharged if internal systems are entirely reliable and characterized by accuracy of content and sensible use. At the same time, one of the most important factors in the selection of a financial institution is the reputed or previous customer service experience offered by a respective service provider. This depends to some extent on the speed at which the provider is able to address customer requests and input.

Application

Santander's application of Scrum outside of the software development environment involves the isolated utilization of some of its Events. For example, Standup meetings are used by non-software teams, and the concept of the S|print, Sprint Goal or Backlog are also exploited. So, while the bank does not always apply Scrum in its entirety, or even to a project aimed at the introduction of a new product, the primary principles of the system, such as the immediacy of its discursive communication or the tools that it provides to strategize forward progress, are made use of in adapted or niche applicati0ons.

Outcome

Santander cite two advantages of using Scrum, or Agile generally, int eh management processes of their operations. These are that:

- It is more responsive
- It is more flexible

The first revolves around the fact that time is not required to the same extent in meeting the changing requirements of the market or addressing the emergence of new technology or products. Organizational responsiveness is increased through the use of Agile techniques. This may be due to the presence of smaller operational teams or units, or the inherent incentive in the Agile philosophy for staff to motivate themselves and to take ownership of that response. This, in turn, encourages a broader awareness of their organization, its market, and their industry environment generally, so that they are far more effective in meeting the challenges of their jobs.

The flexibility of the Scrum (or Agile) approach is obvious and hand hardly needs to be elaborated on. Santander refer to what is known as "mission creep" (or "feature creep"), a term which describes how the ultimate goal of a project can change during its duration, or how a product can start to shift in its features, based on market demand or developer initiative. Tracking competitor developments or market trends I much easier if the product is being developed in stages, or iterations.

In the same way that some large enterprises have adapted Scrum to suit their own style of application or or specific operational requirements,

Santander uses Scrum Events to manage projects that are not based in IT. This adaptation, either of the system itself or the area of its application, indicates how general and salient its underlying philosophy is. The entire Agile movement, in fact, can be described in those terms, and it is in the non-IT applications of its methodologies that is even more apparent.

CHAPTER TEN

Industry and Resources

Scrum has been an established management system for more than 20 years now, so literature and supportive material is not hard to obtain. Those who conduct searches for such matter should take into account the relationship between Scrum and Agile, since the two are sometimes merged in discussions, or the distinction between them is not adequately maintained. As a reminder, Scrum is one methodology in the Agile stable, one which pre-dates the Agile movement and yet shares many of its principles. In seeking information on Scrum, the reader is advised to assign relatively more significance to the names of its co-founders, which are Ken Schwaber and Jeff Sutherland. Students of Scrum are in the fortunate position that the founders of the system are still alive, and still active in the industry, so the seminal sources of its philosophy still deliver opinions on its application or criticism.

That Scrum has been criticized should not be ignored. There are two possible reasons for such criticism. The first is that some people simply prefer to use a different system in coordinating their projects. This is a natural phenomenon in any commercial or even human activity. Where one or more than one method of operation is possible, it is unlikely that there is going to be uniformity in the selection of the desired method. Added to this is the fact that management consultants derive an income through the promotion of one or other system, and if they have acquired a preference during the course of their careers, or if they have deliberately aligned themselves with a particular system (for whatever reason), then they are obviously going to express negative sentiments about other, rival systems.

Secondly, mangers may not always understand how suitable, or otherwise, a system such as Scrum is to their specific purposes. Inappropriate application may result in disappointing results, either of the project or the entire business operation, and the system is then blamed for this outcome. This is a misplaced emphasis, since the failure of the activity or enterprise is more an illustration of its management's deficient expertise than anything else. Above all, it should always be remembered that no management system offers an automatic or autopilot solution to project and business management. It is not enough simply to deploy principles and tools and then hope for a favorable outcome. Any system merely serves as guidance, not as a set of operational instructions, and without the necessary commercial insights and management ability, it is useless.

Industry

The Scrum industry is a semi-official sub-sector of the management environment. There are recognized Scrum qualifications, such as Scrum Master, and these are administered by organizations who are easiest to locate and contact online. The following are some of the more prominent ones.

- scrum.org. This is an enterprise headed by Scrum co-founder Ken Schwaber. It is perhaps the best starting point in inquiries because it is the territory of the system's co-author himself.
- www.scrumfoundation.com
- www.scrumalliance.org

Literature

Over the last 20 years, Scrum has had time to be used, experimented with and commented on. It is not the intention of this author to dictate to the reader what literature they should focus on, or which authors they should maintain loyalty to. The list below provides the titles of some books, but as to the scope and extent of further reading, the reader is advised to determine their own priorities.

- *The Scrum Papers by Jeff Sutherland* – **Free download available**
- *Scrum Primer 2.0 by Pete Deemer, Gabrielle Benefield, Craig Larman and Bas Vodde* – **Free download available** www.scrumfoundation.org
- *Essential Scrum: A Practical Guide tot he most Popular Agile Process by Kenny Rubin*
- *Scrum in Action by Andrew Pham*
- *The Elements of Scrum by Hillary Louise Johnson and Chris Sims*

CONCLUSION

As one of the main approaches in project management, the Agile movement offers a vastly different paradigm to the more linear, structured systems. Its emphasis on people, quality, and staged delivery, or iterative development, ensures that the organization subscribing to its principles maintains heightened responsiveness to the market conditions and and a superior ability to satisfy customer expectations, through the accommodation of more frequent feedback and abstinence from holistic commitment to a long-term final product which may be irrelevant or unsuitable once it is eventually delivered.

Speaking of quality, errors are easier top detect and prevent in Agile methodologies, and the assignment of a designated assessment role to at least one member of the team is a step in that direction. Allowing the customer or end-user access to the development process, such as during the Sprint Review meetings at the end of each Sprint, also enables the latter to provide their input and monitor the progress of the work that they have commissioned, so that the ultimate test, namely the opinion of the customer, is an influence in the development process, and theoretical models of testing or beta-tester feedback , although they may also be used, are consigned to their proper place in product delivery, namely the back seat.

Scrum, as an example of the Agile philosophy, exhibits all f the main principles, and is one of the most popular subsystems in use at present. Supported by the active involvement of its co-founders, |Ken Schwaber and Jeff Sutherland, as well as successful deployment by several large international enterprises, those who make use of it, or are considering doing so, should remember that they may rely on a long tradition of concrete deployment and that they will not struggle to access assistance or supporting material.

Ultimately, the reader should decide for themselves which management system best suits their specific requirements. This can only be done on a casuistic, project-orientated basis, and it is hoped that this e-book, in providing introductory information on Scrum, has served to inform the reader tot eh extent that they are able to make a provisional decision as top what will ensure timeous delivery at the estimated budget.

We really hope that the information provided in this book was valuable to you and that it over delivered on your expectations. Although we like to think we are perfect, we are human and do make mistakes. If for any reason you are not satisfied with your purchase, have any comments/or feedback you would like to share directly with us, please reach us at clydebankpublishing@gmail. com. Additionally, if you would like a refund, you can return the purchase through Amazon up to 7 days after the initial purchase. If you would like a refund after these 7 days, please contact us directly.

Again, we thank you for your business and hope you are satisfied with your purchase. If you are, we would love to receive a positive review from you on the book's product page. We live and die by the support of you, the customer, so we would greatly appreciate it.

ABOUT THE AUTHOR

Ed Stark is a veteran of corporate America with over 20+ years of professional business experience. Ed has held a managerial role in a variety of different industries including but not limited to IT, Software and Energy & Environmental. Ed has been professionally trained in numerous management schools of thought, techniques and methods and is self-taught in several other business related topics.

More recently, Ed's role in the business world has taken a backseat to his love for writing and teaching. A scientific approach that is rooted in the fundamentals, Ed's books act as catalysts that foster the personal and professional development of current and soon to be business professionals. Putting what he has learned in the field onto paper for others to benefit from, Ed hopes his books will teach and inspire individuals in the business world to become better managers, executives and leaders.

PREVIEW OF

"Agile Project Management QuickStart Guide" - By Ed Stark

Chapter 1: Understanding Project Management

The Necessity of Project Management

It is a feature of many economic activities that they cannot be successfully conducted by one person. The need for diverse yet specialized skills, extensive productive hours or simply the sheer volume of administrative procedure translates into larger labor forces and expanded possibilities through collective effort. In many professional teams, no single person has the entire scope of expertise and available time to perform the required tasks so as to effect the desired outcome.

Project management is the term used to refer to the process of coordinating and regulating a collective approach to the execution of a task. The project might be long term in nature, such as the construction of a new high-rise building, or it may be more immediate, such as the repair of an important machine. The extent of the skills required to achieve the targeted result may be far beyond what one person is capable of acquiring during their education or career, while the amount of work involved might necessitate a considerable level of participation from other people. At the same time, synchronizing the immense operational detail that is associated with some projects is hardly possible for a sole individual.

Of course, distributing the scope of responsibility involved in a larger project to more than one person attracts its own related difficulties. Any activity that relies on the commitment and adequate effort of more than one person is subject to obstruction through disloyalty, unreliability or the poor coordination of its component events. For this reason, organizations have tried to establish reliable and standard methods to manage and focus projects, in order to attain the requisite level of cooperation and ensure the success of the collective endeavor.

The scale of a project can be immense. Nowadays, the budgets of national government departments and multinational corporations can run into hundreds of millions of dollars and entail the participation of thousands of employees. The scope of the project's practical consequences can also be enormous.

As an example, The Three Gorges Dam in China, which was completely in the early 2000s, is 660km in length and contains approximately 9 cubic miles of water, weighing 40 billion tons. This mass of water is so substantial that it actually affects the rotation of the earth to a slight yet significant extent, and has shifted the position of the magnetic poles by nearly an inch. Its hydroelectric installation generates an estimated 22 500MW of power (equivalent to about 20 nuclear power reactors).

No one person could possibly have constructed the dam on their own.

Yet in today's world such projects are not merely expressions of nationalist sentiment or aimed at exceptional economic reward. They are entirely necessary in providing amenities to the population and enabling the economic growth and stability that people rely on to survive. The coordination of massive collective efforts is not made necessary by inordinate ambition or ideological misapplication – it is essential to the sustainability of modern existence.

Issues in Project Management

There are certain obvious issues which always arise in the management of collective or group initiatives. Getting a number of people to work together on a single enterprise is not the easiest task in business or society. Anyone who has attempted this in the past should be familiar with that notion. Even a simple activity, such as a sports team or litter-reduction campaign, can be obstructed or delayed to the point that they never materialize.

The first and most basic matter of contention is the reliable participation of everyone in the group. This is harder to ensure in non-professional situations. The employment environment usually translates into a more committed attitude from participants, even if they are not entirely dedicated to their jobs or they do not regard their employment as an area requiring more than the minimum of enthusiasm. However, where there is no remuneration attached to the project, or where there are no penalties for abandonment of the assigned task, loyalty can be extremely hard to secure. This is seen even in cases where significant monetary reward was associated with participation, such as famous music bands which fell apart, or the discarding of litter in public places which, while not a prosecutable offense, is nevertheless a source of displeasure to the community.

Once the group has been identified and their commitment to the common task has been confirmed, the issue of sustained and effective communication becomes apparent. This is particularly so in multinational projects, where participants may never have met in person and cannot afford to congregate in the same geographical location. Modern technology has reduced the challenge presented by this situation, but the ease and efficacy of communication within the team is sometimes still an obstacle to its success, even where all of its members are based in the same office.

It has already been mentioned that one of the primary reasons for using a group approach is to ensure that all the necessary skills are available. The coordination of these skills then becomes a priority for the project manager. Some of them may only be necessary for a short time, while others need to be available for the entire duration of the project and its aftermath. The contemporary proliferation and advanced specialization of skills in some disciplines has resulted in a scarcity of qualified people in certain areas of economic activity. The effective acquisition and direction of these skills is an important role of the project management strategy.

On a practical level, there are also issues to be negotiated. One apprehensive assumption about group activities is that they cost more and they take more time. This is not automatically the case, but then the management of the project needs to be able to counter or eliminate these eventualities. This is especially so where the project has been initiated in a commercial sphere and has a budget and time-frame approved by a paying customer. It may be a source of extreme disappointment if either of these parameters is exceeded, such as when new homeowners have to move into a half-finished house or the project commissioner simply cannot afford any further extension.

Lastly, the customer or end-user, or even the project participants themselves, need to be satisfied with the outcome. The collective activity must actually produce the result that it was supposed to. The measurement of this standard is a source of potential conflict. A long-term and expensive project may result in failure. This may not even be due to any fault of the project team, since varying requirements or changing market conditions can cause the customer to adapt their expectations during the course of the project's duration.

This final issue, in particular, is addressed by the Agile methodologies. As the Agile management paradigm is discussed in the next chapters, it is important to remember the issues that have been raised in this section, so as to observe how it addresses and solves them.

Chapter 2: A History of Agile Project Management

The Agile Alliance

The concept of a standardized or prescribed strategy towards project management is not new. Different organizations or cultures may have practiced their own endemic methods in regulating large labor forces or assigning resources to the projects that they engaged in. However, it was only since the middle of the 1950s that the concept began to be regarded as a more formal discipline in itself and attracted its official terminology. At present, it is taken seriously in commerce and elsewhere, as evidenced by, for example, the Association of Project Management (APM) in the UK or the American Society for the Advancement of Project Management (ASAPM).

To the extent that project management methods already existed by the turn of the 21st century, Agile Project Management is based on or a response to several of them. The formulation and subsequent promotion of a discrete and self-contained management methodology is therefore not a novelty per se. That it draws on existing systems of both project and business management is not surprising either.

Agile Project Management (or Agile for short) was devised within the software industry. The process of inventing new software is known specifically as "developing" it. The initiators of the Agile doctrine were all software developers. This is possibly why it has such a strong association with the IT sector. Proponents have made the assertion that it is applicable to any industry, and there is literature examining how this has happened in practice. Its potential deployment in activities outside of IT will be discussed further in later chapters of this e-book.

In early 2000, correspondence between the eventual role-players was started about project management techniques. This initial interest blossomed into a formal conference in Chicago in 2001. There, 17 professionals in the software industry thrashed out a new method, based on their experience in their respective preferred alternatives. At this meeting, they composed the various statements that have become synonymous with the Agile movement.

Firstly, they identified what are regarded as the three erroneous assumptions in project management:

- The first flawed assumption is that it is possible to plan such a large project.

- The second flawed assumption is that it is possible to protect against late changes.

- The third flawed assumption is that it even makes sense to lock in big projects early.

As you can see, these three issues all highlight the point raised at the end of the previous chapter, namely that the objective of a project (or the end-user's expectations) can change during the course of its execution. This makes it impossible for the project team to provide a satisfactory result. The first assumption on the list, on the other hand, is an allusion to the immensity of some projects and how they are not amenable to a rigid and detailed framework or forecasting. Even a simple job like painting a house depends on stable weather. How much more so, then, the construction of a dam spanning an entire mountain range? The unpredictable nature of the project environment is also encompassed by the four primary principles that the meeting ascertained. These are:

- Individuals and interactions over processes and tools

- Working software over comprehensive documentation

- Customer collaboration over contract negotiation

- Responding to change over following a plan

With the proviso that: That is, while there is value in the items on the right, we value the items on the left more. The last item is particularly of note here, but the others also serve to illustrate the emphasis on people instead of procedure (the first item), on the efficacy of the end result rather than the bureaucratic administration of its development and presence in the market (the second item) and on customer service and satisfaction over impersonal, disinterested business practice (item three).

It should be stated that the emphasis on reducing the administration associated with a project (its bureaucracy or "comprehensive documentation) sometimes attracts the adjective "lightweight" in the context of Agile (as opposed to the "heavyweight" systems that encompass extensive administration and management structures) In trying to establish these principles as the elements of a project management strategy in practice, the meeting generated the following 12 Principles of Agile Software:

- Our highest priority is to satisfy the customer through early and continuous delivery of valuable software.
- Welcome changing requirements, even late in development. Agile processes harness change for the customer's competitive advantage.
- Deliver working software frequently, from a couple of weeks to a couple of months, with a preference to the shorter timescale.
- Business people and developers must work together daily throughout the project.
- Build projects around motivated individuals. Give them the environment and support they need, and trust them to get the job done.
- The most efficient and effective method of conveying information to and within a development team is face-to-face conversation.

- Working software is the primary measure of progress.

- Agile processes promote sustainable development. The sponsors, developers, and users should be able to maintain a constant pace indefinitely.

- Continuous attention to technical excellence and good design enhances agility.

- Simplicity – the art of maximizing the amount of work not done – is essential.

- The best architectures, requirements, and designs emerge from self-organizing teams.

- At regular intervals, the team reflects on how to become more effective, then tunes and adjusts its behavior accordingly.

(www.agilemanifesto.org)

This list of principles is known in the industry as the Agile Manifesto and has been officially published on the website of the Agile Alliance, which consists of the original 17 members who drafted it. They are, in no particular order:

Kent Beck, Mike Beedle, Arie van Bennekum, Alistair Cockburn, Ward Cunningham, Martin Fowler, James Grenning, Jim Highsmith, Andrew Hunt, Ron Jeffries, Jon Kern, Brian Marick, Robert C. Martin, Steve Mellor, Ken Schwaber, Jeff Sutherland, Dave Thomas

There is no need to enter into a detailed analysis of these individuals or their careers in the IT industry. What is important to note is that some of them represent the most prominent existing management paradigms at the time. These were Extreme Programming, Adaptive Software Development, Feature-Driven Development, Pragmatic Programming, Crystal, SCRUM, and DSDM. Some of these are either closely associated with Agile or are regarded as its subsidiary methodologies. What is also obvious from the names alone is that they are related to software development.

One contributor who does merit individual mention is Jim Highsmith, who has gone on to create a reputation for himself as the leading authority on the Agile Project Management methodology. Others, such as Kent Beck and Alistair Cockburn, formulated Extreme Programming (XP) and Crystal methodology respectively.

Motivation

The desire to establish a new, more effective or otherwise improved project management system in the software industry was based on advertised and substantial dissatisfaction with existing methods. This was perhaps due to the expansion of the IT industry, both in terms of its scale and range of application, or merely because the nature of its product makes it the territory for this type of experimentation.

By the year 2000, the internet, software and computer technology in general were starting to be regarded as the machinery of the future, the equipment that would take not only local industries but the developing global economy into the next century. People may not remember the Y2K crisis (the phenomenon that arose as a result of the inability of some software to process more than two digits for the year in a date, rendering it useless on 1 January 2000), or how excited economists and other commercial observers became with the introduction of IT into each new sphere of economic activity. But the overarching sentiment was one of expectation, and all the sci-fi style imaginative prediction that goes with it in such instances.

With the IT industry being required to supply solutions to so many different markets, and on such a massive scale, a refined or even entirely new management approach was a likely priority, especially one which is so uniquely suited to the industry itself. As an example, Windows 95, an earlier Microsoft operating system (which some younger readers may have to Google to identify), sold 40 million copies in its first year. Microsoft's latest offering, Windows 8, reached 100 million copies in its first six months.

There is one fundamental characteristic of software and its development which may make it susceptible to trouble. This is more so in connection with the already outlined unstable nature of a project and its targeted results. It is what the industry terms "uncertainty". The development of new software is uncertain in that its ultimate desired functionality cannot be determined until it is in use by the customer.

Sometimes, the end-user's expectations change once they are using it, since they may realize new possibilities or receive more decisive feedback from their own target market. In this way, the software developer is tasked with creating a product that is satisfactory, but which at the same time has to subscribe to the potentially shifting requirements of its commissioner. This is known as "scope creep" and the opportunity that it presents for failure, frustration or miscommunication is therefore obvious.

Prior to the advent of Agile, the other management protocols revolved around two basic approaches:

- **Waterfall:** this one is the most popularly mentioned in conjunction with Agile, and is either seen as an opposing methodology or somehow inferior to the latter. It involves developing the software according to a prior plan or determined framework of activity, like the stages in the rapids of a waterfall. It is sometimes referred to as "plan-driven".

- **Spiral, rapid prototyping, evolutionary delivery, and incremental delivery:** all of these entail the production of pieces of the ultimate product at a time, for the customer to experiment with and provide a response to. They are sometimes described as "agile", i.e. as opposed to the execution of a premeditated plan.

The incremental or phased nature of the second approach seems more compatible with the development of software, since it serves to lessen or even alleviate the uncertainty that is sometimes innate to the process. (For a more comprehensive comparison of Waterfall to Agile, see Chapter 9. This distinction is critical in understanding how organizations go about choosing which approach to use.) In assessing the various sub-methodologies that have arisen under the Agile umbrella, it is important to remember what preceded it and how they have contributed to its present structure and application.

MORE BY ED STARK

Project Management For Beginners:

Proven Project Management Methods To Complete

Projects With Time & Money To Spare

Author: Ed Stark

Link: http://bit.ly/project_success

Agile Project Management QuickStart Guide:

A Simplified Beginners Guide To Agile Project Management

Author: Ed Stark

 Link: http://bit.ly/agile_quickstart

Lean Six Sigma QuickStart Guide:

A Simplified Beginners Guide To Lean Six Sigma

Author: Ed Stark

Link: http://bit.ly/lean-sixsigma

Made in the USA
Lexington, KY
14 January 2015